index

graphic effects and typographic treatments

D0171836

index

graphic effects and typographic treatments

JIM KRAUSE

NORTH LIGHT BOOKS
Cincinnati, Ohio
www.howdesign.com

About the Author

Jim Krause has worked as a designer in the Pacific Northwest since the 1980's. He has produced award-winning work for clients large and small, including Microsoft, McDonald's, Washington Apples, Bell Helicopter, Paccar/Kenworth, Northern Trust and Seattle Public Schools.

Published by North Light Books, an imprint of F&W Publications, Inc., 1507 Dana Avenue, Cincinnati, Ohio 45207. (800) 289-0963. First edition.

Other fine North Light Books are available from your local bookstore, art supply store or direct from the publisher. Visit our Web site at www.howdesign.com for more resources for graphic designers.

04 03 02 01   5

Library of Congress Cataloging-in-Publication Data

Krause, Jim, 1962–
    Idea index / Jim Krause.
      p. cm.
    ISBN 1-58180-046-0 (alk. paper)
     1. Graphic design (Typography)—Handbooks, manuals, etc. I. Title.

  Z246 . K8 2000
  686.2'252–dc21   99-057574

Edited by Lynn Haller and Linda Hwang
Production coordinated by John Peavler
Interior designed by Jim Krause
Cover by Jim Krause

Thank you
Evan, Debra, Jenni, Steven and Kathy,
for giving me what I needed
to start and finish this book.

Table of Contents, Section I

Table of Contents, Section II

Introduction

THE CREATIVE RESERVE

Consciously and unconsciously, visual artists constantly add to their creative reservoir with concepts and images from everyday life. Fresh combinations and adaptations of these elements are drawn from this reserve whenever an artist searches for a solution to a project.

Among these solutions, only those that are unique and original among current media are likely to catch a viewer's eye. Successful artists and designers are those who are able to consistently find these images while maintaining an awareness of current trends. And since new solutions are often drawn from reconfigurations of old material (these solutions, in turn, reinforcing or establishing trends of their own), it could be said that the most effective designers and illustrators are those who have the deepest creative reserve, and the greatest skill at evolving existing concepts and images into fresh creations.

It would be impossible for an artist to scan the content of their creative reserve every time he or she searches for a solution to a new project. Certain useful ideas float to the surface, while others remain hidden. This difficulty in retrieving the right idea(s) at the right time is a significant obstacle between an artist and an effective solution— a difficulty compounded by the pressure of approaching deadlines.

ENTER *IDEA INDEX*

While doing nothing to change the actual creative process—a process carried out uniquely by every artist—*Idea Index* puts it in "fast forward": supercharging the search for a unique and interesting solution. By placing hundreds of visual and conceptual suggestions directly before the artist's eyes and mind, *Idea Index* stimulates, quickens and expands the creative process. Simply put, this book is a tool that stocks the creative reservoir, brings useful ideas to the surface and offers the spark needed to make a good idea *great*.

WHO *IDEA INDEX* IS FOR, AND WHEN TO USE IT

Idea Index is for graphic designers, illustrators, art directors and any professionals involved in the creation of visual media. Students will also find this book very useful not only for expanding their creative awareness, but also as an illustrated resource of current graphic techniques and styles.

Use *Idea Index* at the beginning of a project to get ideas stirring or later on, to expand a page or two of thumbnail sketches; use it as "mental drain-opener" when the creative juices have slowed or stopped flowing; use it to get things moving during group brainstorming sessions; thumb through the pages during downtime to "top off" the creative reservoir.

HOW TO USE IT

There are as many ways to use *Idea Index* as there are people who use it. The following two pages describe, in a very general way, a sequence that could be followed in search of ideas and inspiration leading toward a solution.

1) **The project is defined.** Logo, brochure, book, Web site, poster, package design, illustration, etc. Budget and timeline considerations are taken into account.

2) **The audience is targeted.** What kinds of messages and images will this audience react to favorably? What types of media reach them the most directly? What kinds of images are they already exposed to? Should trends be followed or not?

3) **Brainstorm.** What content could the image and message contain? Make lists and sketches of potentially useful subject matter, phrases, color combinations and graphic styles. There are no bad ideas at this point; the search will narrow itself later as the most effective ideas reveal themselves.

4) **Open *Idea Index.*** The designer, illustrator or art director, seeking to expand and/or refine the search for a solution, opens to the appropriate section (Graphic Effects or Typographic Treatments) of *Idea Index.* Looking at a page, the designer considers:

Could this concept or effect be applied?
If not, *turn to another page.* If so, *consider:*

Would it reinforce the message?
If not, *turn to another page.* If so, *consider:*

What are some variations of this idea?
Endless variations could be applied to every topic presented in this book. To assist in the search for an effective solution, each page of visual suggestions is accompanied by text that offers additional brainstorming material. This text, like the illustrations, is meant to offer fuel for creativity rather than specific answers. For this reason, the text is intentionally sparse, vague and sometimes self-contradictory.

Also consider:

Should additional concepts be sought or effects added?
Designers may, at this point, add ideas of their own, continue turning pages of *Idea Index* or pursue a specific solution. Determining the next step depends on whether or not the designer feels that additional elements or refinement would increase the effectiveness of the piece.

Using this book, an artist might choose to scan every page—or only a few—in search of useful material. The book could be viewed from start to finish, finish to start or randomly. And naturally, when a promising chain of thought or the refinement of an image calls for more attention, the artist will set this book aside.

EXAMPLE PAGES
In addition to visual and textual brainstorming material, *Idea Index* includes eleven spreads that offer examples of how concepts from this book can be applied, step-by-step demonstrations of useful techniques and further suggestions for finding pathways to creative solutions.

WHY *IDEA INDEX* IS MOSTLY BLACK AND WHITE
The color scheme of *Idea Index* has been kept as simple and non-distracting as possible since colors can attract or repel a viewer, regardless of the content of an image. Additionally, it is worth noting that all of the art presented in this book has been created using readily available illustration, photo manipulation, 3-D rendering, and page make-up software along with a 600 dpi desktop scanner.

It is sincerely hoped that *Idea Index* will prove an invaluable tool in helping designers design, illustrators illustrate and art directors direct art.

SECTION I

GRAPHIC EFFECTS

SECTION I
GRAPHIC EFFECTS

Every visual project begins as a blank page. Effective artists are those best able to find a unique and interesting way to fill the emptiness.

Section I of *Idea Index* features visual and conceptual suggestions intended to spark the viewer's imagination during the search for an effective solution.

Three subjects were chosen to illustrate the sixty-seven topics featured in this section: a *light bulb* (symbol of creativity), a *bolt of lightning* (signifying energy) and an *electrical cord* (the link between bulb and bolt). Limiting the subjects to three common items also provides evidence of the vast number of potential solutions that exist in the search for an effective portrayal of a theme.

The effects illustrated are, of course, meant to be applied to subject matter of the viewer's choosing. The effects could be applied individually, or in combination with others, to photos, illustrations, graphics or text. A solution might be inspired by a single image, a combination of several or through an unexpected chain reaction sparked by a picture or text. Sometimes images from this book will rebound against the mind of a viewer and result in a successful solution far removed from these pages. *Anything goes.*

The viewer is encouraged to combine the concepts found in this book with their own creativity in search of solutions that will please both themselves and their client.

Action

Add movement to an image.

Place a symbol of action within an image.

Present the image itself as a symbol of action.

Contrast an active and a static image.

Move, stop
Up, down
Left, right
Assemble, explode
Whirl
Zoom
Bend
Squeeze
Twist
Shake
Fly

Bitmap

Create a bitmapped image by lowering
resolution settings.

Experiment with a variety of settings.

Imitate a bitmapped image by creating
an icon based on a grid.

Contrast a smooth high-resolution image with
a coarse bitmapped image.

Bitmap an entire image, or only part.

Bitmap a halftone, color photo, black-and-white
image or type element.

Use a bitmapped image as a focal point, or as an
indistinct background image.

*Bitmapped images often convey a look of
technology. Is this relevant to the intended
message and audience?*

Bitmap

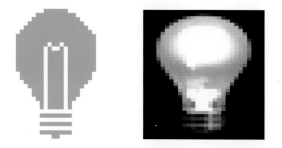

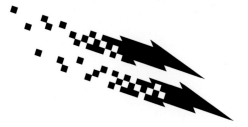

Blueprint

*Would an "unfinished" image convey
the message best?*

Sketch with pencil, pen, charcoal or chalk.

Experiment with different paper and backgrounds.

Create an image with drawing/painting software,
then roughen it using image filters and combine with
a scanned paper (or other) background.

Combine a blueprint with an image of the
actual object.

Leonardo da Vinci
Technical drawing
Drafting

Blueprint

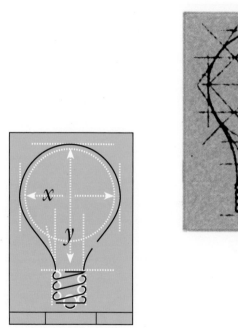

Blur

Blur to convey motion or emotion.

Blur to create a distinctive graphic.

Contrast a blurred image with a sharp image.

Experiment with the effect of different blur filters.

Blur a selected portion of an image.

Blur an entire image or page.

Use a blurred image as a backdrop.

Blur an image until it is barely recognizable.

Blur

Brush

Step away from the computer; clear a space
for paper and ink.

Experiment with a variety of brushes and surfaces.

Consider using a new brush, an old brush, a piece
of wood or crumpled paper, a sponge or wire brush.
Paint with a toothbrush.

Achieve a spontaneous look by working quickly.
Render the subject many times and select the best,
or cut and paste elements from several images to
create a single piece of finished art.

Allow "mistakes" and splatter.

Create the image using software and
electronic brushes.

Note examples of good brushwork.

Brush

Cartoon

Some ideas virtually beg to be portrayed in
cartoon form.

A cartoon might be humorous, whimsical or serious.

Cartoons allow for a fanciful presentation of an idea.

Cartoons are hard for a viewer to resist.

Use cartoons exclusively, or combine with other
kinds of images.

Look for samples of contemporary and/or traditional
styles of cartoon illustration.

Funny
Serious
Editorial
Modern
Old style
Sunday comics

Cartoon

Childlike

Draw like a child.

Create an image that appeals to children.

Consider using crayon, chalk, charcoal, paint, finger-paint, stamps, cut paper or collage.

Choose the best from several quickly drawn images.

Draw with your "opposite" hand.

Ask a child to draw a specific image for you; use as is, or model your version after the child's.

Combine childlike scribbles with a precise graphic.

Childlike

Collage

Cut or tear images from printed material
(be aware of copyright rules).

Cut and paste using glue or software.

Use a collage to express multiple messages, or to
more completely express a single message.

Assemble several different images of
the same subject.

Use a collage as a focal point, or as a background.

Use any combination of photos, illustrations,
graphics, fabric, type.

Paint or draw on top of a collage.

Colorful
Plain
Simple
Complex
Similar or contrasting styles

Collage

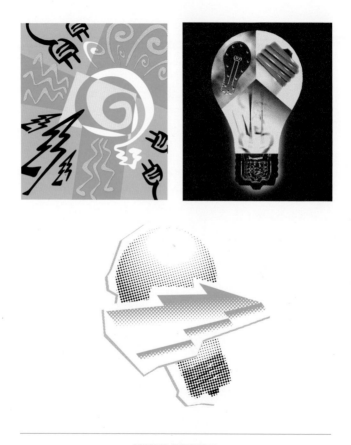

Competing Background

Ignore the "rules" about clarity
and legibility; allow visual competition between
foreground and background images.

Consider complex photographic images,
illustrations, computer-generated lines or graphics
or typographic elements.

Pattern
Multiple layers
Op art
Pop culture
Confusion
Eye games
Motion sickness

Competing Background

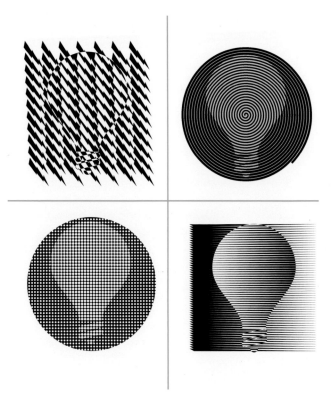

Contrast in Shading

Contrast attracts attention.

Contrast can be stark or subtle.

Explore variations.

Reverse one image from another.

Reverse a light image from a dark background.

Place a dark image over a light background.

Combine a contrast in shading with a contrast
in weight or size.

Black
White
Complementary colors
Yin-yang
Light tones
Loud
Quiet

Contrast in Shading

Contrast in Size

A large image is hard to ignore.

A small image, surrounded by inactive space,
also draws attention.

Place a small image within, or next to, a large image.

Fill a page with a large image; follow it with a page
containing an image that is very small.

Combine a contrast in size with a contrast
in shading or weight.

Go beyond a page's boundaries.

Go too far.

Large
Very, very large
Small
Barely visible
Shout
Whisper

Contrast in Size

Contrast in Weight

Contrast a thin line with a heavy line, object or mass.

Investigate the effects that various line weights have
on a graphic's appearance.

A large contrast in weights can bring interest
to a graphic that might seem plain if rendered with
lines of a consistent weight.

Combine a contrast in weight with a contrast
in size or shading.

Fat
Thin
Busy
Plain
Ornate
Simple

Contrast in Weight

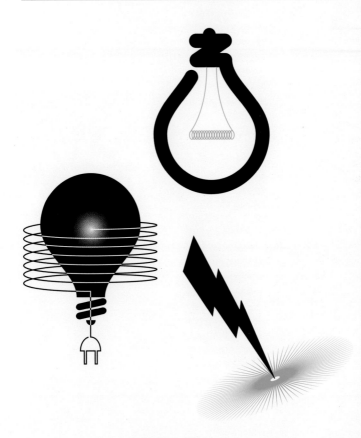

AN EXAMPLE

This book can be used to add speed and depth to the search for a creative solution.

The three designs featured here were created after searching the pages of this book for concepts that could be applied to the visual and typographic elements. Combinations of these concepts were explored, sketches made and designs rendered.

The concepts used are listed with each image.

A similar example is featured on page 200. Also see "Brainstorm," page 66.

MOUNTAIN
SUN
W ✱ E ✱ A ✱ R

Crop

Cut or hide part(s) of an image.

Crop to present a subject in an unusual way.

Crop an image to make room for others.

Crop using a line, shape, border or page's edge.

Crop using the boundaries of another image, graphic or type element.

Crop only a small amount from the image.

Allow only a small amount of the image to remain after cropping.

How much of the image can be cropped before it becomes unrecognizable?

Crop

Crude

A crude style can convey an informal, playful feel.

A crude style can convey deterioration and tension.

A crude style often appeals to a younger audience.

Illustrate in a crude style, or create a crude *look*, by applying image filters to a photo, illustration, graphic or text.

An image can be very rough, or only slightly so.

Cut paper
Tattered edges
Quickly drawn
Out of register
Aged
Weathered
Childlike

Crude

Cut and Paste

You do not need a great deal of training to cut and paste.

Cut and paste to quickly create an interesting image.

Cut and paste using real paper and images.

Cut and paste using software.

Tear instead of cutting.

Experiment with the arrangement of elements.

Paste one image over another.

Preschool
Collage
Layer
Photo
Illustration
Graphic
Type

Cut and Paste

Damage

Photograph a damaged object, or damage an object,
then photograph it.

Imitate damage by applying image filters to a photo,
illustration, graphic or type.

Create an illustration that looks damaged.

Crack
Chip
Tear
Burn
Weather
Fold
Crumple
Photocopy
Tornado
Volcano
War
Violence

Damage

Deform

Deform an image "by hand" or with image filters.

Deform to convey meaning or action, or to bring attention to an image.

Explore software capabilities.

Could this message be strengthened by a subtle or not-so-subtle deformation of the image?

Bend
Twist
Ripple
Melt
Push
Pull
Flatten
Explode

Deform

Dither

A dithered image is made up of tiny stippled dots.

An image is dithered through darkroom techniques, or with the use of software.

Different resolution settings affect the look of a dithered image.

Dithered images can be saved as relatively small computer files since they contain no grey or color information.

Combine or overlay a regular photographic image with a dithered image.

Experiment with the addition of color or tone.

Dither

Doodle

Almost everyone doodles.

A doodle is sometimes more interesting than a "real" illustration.

Doodles can be simple or elaborate.

Doodles can add commentary to an image.

Doodle pictures. Doodle words.

Doodle *over* pictures or words.

Do a bunch of doodles. Pick a favorite.

Doodle with pencil, pen, lipstick, ink, paint or spraypaint.

Sketch
Decorate
Scribble
Vandalize

Doodle

Drop Shadow

The drop shadow can be a surprisingly simple means
of making an image more interesting.

A drop shadow can be realistic, or can be presented
as a simple, hard-edged gray tone.

A drop shadow can add depth to
a two-dimensional image.

Shadows can darken a mood, or convey
a look of sunshine.

Many software programs feature the ability to add
a drop shadow to an image.

Light source
Realistic
Graphic
Flat
Perspective
Dark
Light

Drop Shadow

Emboss, Bas Relief

Press in. Push out.

Be subtle or bold.

Embossing can convey a look of elegance.

Emboss an image from within another's form.

Experiment with different ways of imitating an
embossed look two-dimensionally.

Use a 3-D rendering program to create a
dimensional image.

Paper
Stone
Marble
Metal
Wood
Cement
Clay
Paper sculpture

Emboss, Bas Relief

Era

Style can imply era.

Subject matter can imply era.

Look at history and/or art history books.

Look at posters from another era.

Are certain time periods currently in fashion?

*Are certain time periods appropriate to convey your
subject, or to communicate with your audience?*

Prehistoric
Egyptian
Middle Ages
Renaissance
Industrial Age
Atomic Age
Modern
Futuristic
Revolution

Era

Fade

Fade an image to create interest, or to allow room for other images.

Fade to "nothing," or lighten only a portion of an image.

Fade all or part of an image.

Fade or blur edges.

Fade to convey movement.

Contrast the direction of fades within two adjoining graphics.

Fade gradually.

Fade abruptly.

Fade

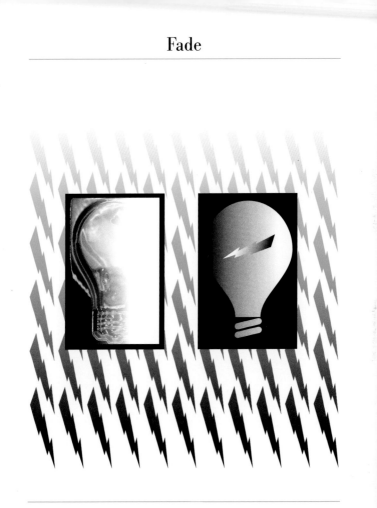

Fill with Image

Fill a silhouette with a
photo, illustration, graphic or type.

Combine multiple ideas in this way.

Feature styles that are similar, or ones that contrast.

Fill a graphic with images of itself.

Keep it simple, or intentionally create
visual confusion.

Fill with Image

BRAINSTORM

Intriguing subject matter often lies at the foundation of a striking image. A good way to begin the search for interesting visual themes is through the use of words. Shown here is a method of using words and lists as a source of inspiration.

Imagine that a client has requested a graphic image that incorporates a human element and an element that conveys "light and enlightenment."

In search of useful visual and conceptual material, two sets of lists are made: objects and qualities that relate to light, and those relating to humanity. The lists evolve freely as the search progresses; sketches and notes are made as interesting combinations among words are found.

Stay in "search mode" until the lists are fairly exhausted, then begin to refine ideas and pursue specific solutions.

Remember, there are no bad ideas when brainstorming. Focus on quantity now, quality later.

HUMANITY

(objects)	(qualities)
people	walk
faces	run
heads	play
eyes	gesture
features	jump
hands	dance
individual	emotion
group	happy
crowd	sad
couple	love
clothing	speak
eyeglasses	touch
hat	embrace
gloves	
shoes	

LIGHT

(objects)	(qualities)
sun	bright
moon	dim
stars	glare
lightbulb	shadow
flashlight	beam
beacon	flare
searchlight	radiate
spotlight	white
lighthouse	colored
chandelier	spectrum
candle	prismatic
flame	
torch	
fire	

Fill with Pattern

Fill a graphic with a pattern.

A pattern can be hand-drawn,
or computer-generated.

Use a pattern of photos, illustrations, graphics
or type.

*Should the pattern complement, or contrast with,
the graphic it fills?*

*Should the pattern be more visually powerful than
the graphic it fills?*

Investigate the patterns used on fabric.

Stark
Subtle
Paisley
Herringbone
Quilt
Freeform

Fill with Pattern

Form with Pattern

Use a pattern or repetitive image to form and/or
define the boundaries of a graphic.

Circumscribe the boundary of a graphic with
a repetitive series of images.

*What kind of pattern would best relate to the style
and message of the overall image?*

Choose pattern elements that are relevant to the
message of the graphic being defined.

Choose pattern elements that contrast with the
message of the graphic being defined.

Simple
Complex
Colorful
Plain

Form with Pattern

Form with Type

Doubly emphasize a message by forming an image with relevant text.

Investigate font choices.

Which font reinforces the message best?

Form an entire image using type.

Create an image by highlighting a specific pattern of characters within a text block.

Form or fill a portion of an image with type.

Use letters and/or punctuation marks.

Use a single font, or several.

Form with Type

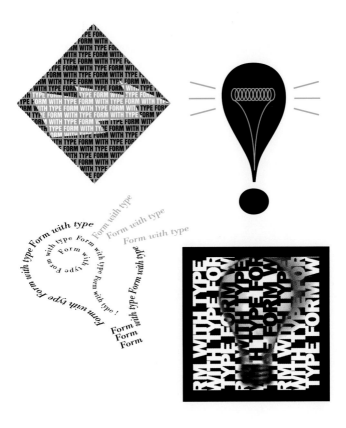

Fragment

Explode the image.

Fragment using image filters.

Fragment using a utility knife.

Fragment by dropping.

Illustrate the fragmentation as a sequence of images.

TNT
Firecracker
Lightning
Paper shredder
Sudden explosion
Step-by-step explosion
Broken glass
Torn or cut paper

Fragment

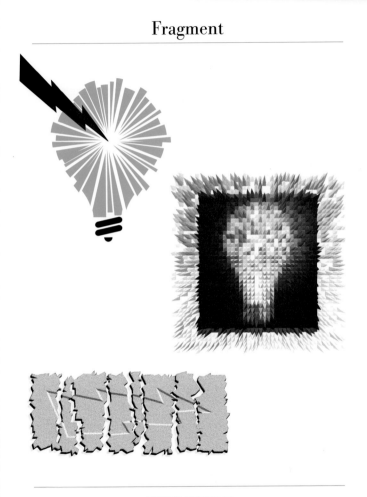

Frame

A frame or border can complement
an image's message or tone.

A frame or border can add a message of its own.

A simple border can bring order to a chaotic image.

An active border can add energy to a plain image.

Frame an image with a series of others.

Frame with a line or set of lines.

Use pseudo-photographic edge treatments.

Don't allow the frame or border to overshadow the
image within (unless by intention).

Square, circle, triangle, ellipse
Rough, smooth
Bold, thin
Black, white, color, tone
Busy, plain
Ornate, subtle

Frame

Ghost

An image could be ghosted to impart mood.

Ghost an image to allow others to overprint clearly.

Experiment with the limits of visibility.

Place a crisp image over a ghosted background.

Place a ghosted image over a crisp background.

Place a ghosted image over a ghosted background.

Experiment with image filters.

Ghost a photo, illustration, graphic or type.

Dark against dark
Light against light
Light against dark
Background
Foreground
Mood
Blur
Soft

Ghost

Glow

The illusion of light.

Highlight a single element within an image by adding glow.

Make everything glow.

Investigate image filters and settings that create glow.

Soft light
Harsh light
Dark or light background
Backlit
Fluorescent
Enthusiasm
Mystery

Glow

Graffiti

Add a note of anarchy.

Imitate graffiti using ink, paint, spraypaint,
or software and mouse.

Overprint photos, illustrations, graphic images or
type with images of graffiti.

"Deface" an entire page with graffiti.

Look at real graffiti for inspiration.

Use images of real graffiti.

Hire a graffiti artist.

Spraypaint
Dripping paint
Brick, concrete
Vandalism
Revolution
Social commentary
Public poetry

Graffiti

Halftone, Enlarged Line

A linear screen is sometimes used to create a halftone image. Enlarging this screen to the point of visibility can produce interesting results.

Experiment with resolution settings and screen angles.

See the following page spread for a variation of this idea.

Old linocut images
Television images
Movement
Direction

Halftone, Enlarged Line

Halftone, Visible Dot

Normally, the dots in a halftone are invisible to
the naked eye. Sufficiently lowering the resolution
setting (also referred to as "using a *coarse screen*")
will result in an image with visible dots.

Experiment with various resolution settings.

A plain image can become visually intriguing when
presented using a coarse screen.

Enlarge printed halftone images until dots are visible
and allow the natural imperfections to show.

Use an extreme enlargement of a halftone as a
backdrop for other images.

Resolution settings can be varied for both black-and-
white and color images.

*See the previous page spread for a
variation of this idea.*

Halftone, Visible Dot

Human Connotation

Humans relate to images of humans.

Humans or human features.

Things that humans do.

Could a human connotation enhance the message?

Combine or contrast a human element with a
nonhuman or nonliving element.

Many possibilities. Brainstorm thoroughly.

Person, people
Face, eye, mouth, ear, nose
Senses
Hands, feet
Male, female, unisex
Reproduction
Family
Speak, dance, run, stand, play, work, love

Human Connotation

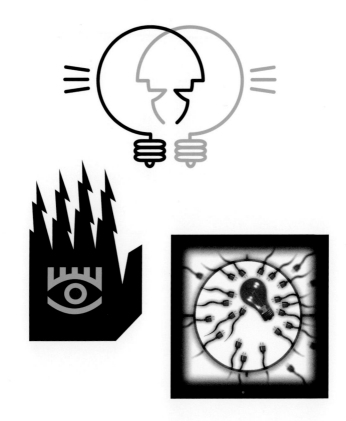

Intricate

Artistry, intelligence, depth, thoroughness.

Contrast an intricate image with a simple image or background.

Combine several intricate images.

Layers of meaningful, informative images.

Layers of frivolous decoration.

Doodle or draw until there is room for no more.

Embellishment
Decoration
Schematic drawing
Cutaway rendering
Pattern
Collage
Assemblage

Intricate

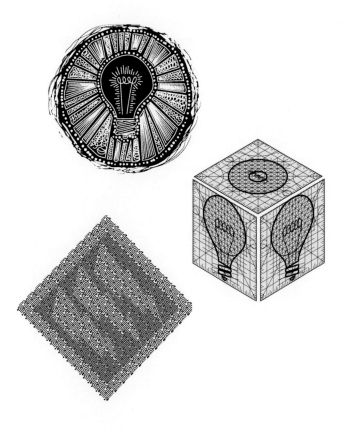

SIMPLIFICATION

Most of the concepts featured in this section of this book have to do with the process of simplification and the stylization that results when an image is reduced to its essential elements. Simplifying an image, whether slightly or significantly, is the core process by which many logos and graphic images are created.

Exploration and experimentation are essential to the search for effective simplification/stylization. Investigate as many possibilities as time allows.

Don't be afraid to oversimplify a subject while looking for a solution—you can always "re-add" elements or detail if an image becomes unrecognizable.

An eye, realistically rendered.

A collection of eyes, some rendered more sim-ply than others. Note how the process of simplification lends itself to stylistic inter-pretation along the way.

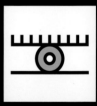

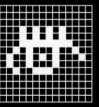

Linocut

Print from carved linoleum, wood, eraser,
cardboard or potato.

Experiment with inks and printing surfaces.

Look at a book about linocuts or block printing.

Imitate a linocut using software.

A linocut can be printed in a single color, or several.

Allow less-than-perfect registration between colors.

Traditional
Modern
Nineteenth-century naturalist book
Grammar-school art class
Rubber stamp

Linocut

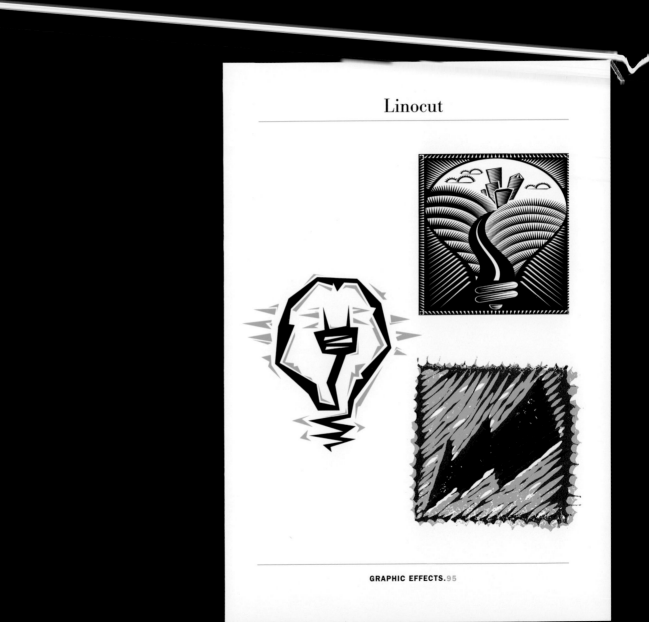

Mask, Stencil

Paint, draw, scribble or shade within a stencil.

Paint, draw, scribble or shade outside a mask.

Use a stenciled or masked image over a
photo, illustration, graphic or type.

Be neat. Be messy.

Use layers of masks or stencils.

Use real stencils or masks to create artwork.

Imitate stencils or masks using software
and/or image filters.

Mask, Stencil

Material

Surprise the viewer: render an object as though it were made from an unexpected material.

Defy reality.

Vast possibilities. Brainstorm.

Which materials could be used to emphasize the subject's message?

Investigate the capabilities of 3-D rendering software.

Metal
Wood
Stone
Glass
Organic
Liquid, solid, molten
Textured, smooth
Shiny, dull
Hard, soft
Transparent, translucent, opaque
Three-dimensional, two-dimensional

Material

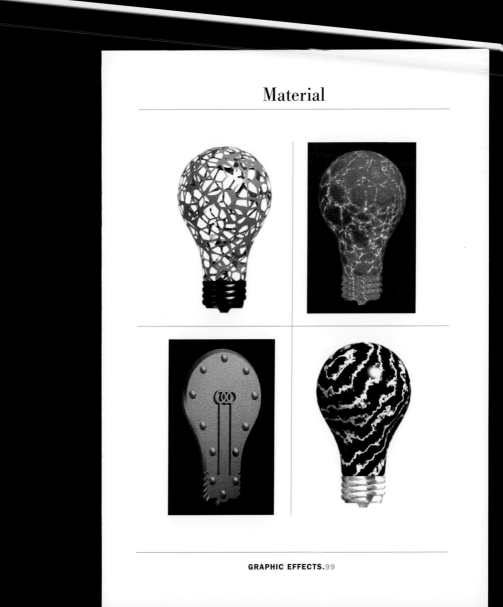

Minimal

How much of an image could be "left out" and still retain meaning for the viewer?

Minimalize to focus attention.

Minimalize to create an impression of order and cleanliness.

Experiment with degrees of simplification.

*Over*simplify an image, then gradually add to it until it is once again recognizable.

Surround the image with inactive space.

Surround the image with clutter.

Combine the look of minimalization with other techniques and concepts.

Minimal

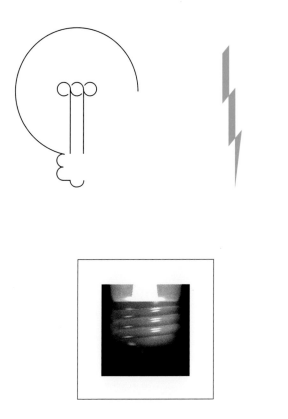

Mood

Mood is subjective.

*Who is the audience for this piece? How could a
specific mood be conveyed to them?*

Trust your instinct.

Trust the instinct of others.

Present contrasting moods through
contrasting images.

Typography also imparts and/or enforces mood.

Joy, sadness
Laughter, tears
Enthusiasm, melancholy
Hope, despair
Light, dark
Loneliness
Gray
Blur
Soft
Hard

Mood

enlighten

me

Multimedia

Combine a variety of media to create an
intriguing image.

*Look through this book. Which styles and
methods of rendering could be combined to create
an interesting conglomerate?*

Choose styles that are greatly different.

Choose styles that are closely related.

Photo	Type	Layer
Paint	Handwriting	Ornament
Ink	Calligraphy	Symbol
Silhouette	Multiple fonts	Graffiti
Sketch	Splatter	Frame
Drawing	Scientific	Childlike
Thumbnail	Stamp	Cut or tear
Television image	Pattern	Neat, chaotic
Collage	Overlap	Blur, sharpen

Multimedia

Multiple Outline

Surround or fill an image with lines.

Precise lines.

Loosely drawn lines.

Experiment with various line weights and tones.

Use a single line weight, or several.

Lines could transform as they radiate from an image.

Photograph or imitate neon.

Multiple Outline

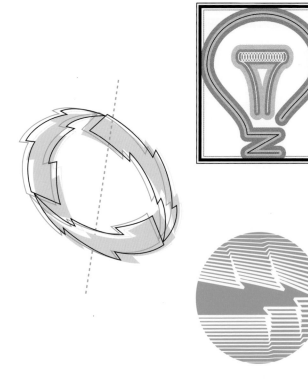

Nature

Images from nature can convey growth, life, change, death or destruction.

Could your subject benefit from an association with the natural world?

Create an image featuring elements from nature.

Look at a plant or seed catalog.

Look outside. Go for a walk.

Contrast items from nature with machines or other man-made devices.

Create tension with images of nature in distress.

Plants, animals, fish, insects, birds
Earth, sea, sky
Sun, moon, heavens
Life, death
Growth, decay

Nature

Negative

In some cases, a negative image enforces a message
most effectively.

Combine a positive and a negative image.

Black-and-white negative.

Color negative.

Add additional effects to a negative image
with filters.

Create a negative from a threshold or posterized
image (see pages 160 and 161).

Negative

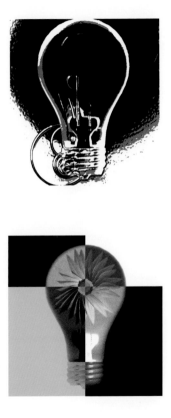

Odd

Combine seemingly unrelated images or ideas to communicate a message or attract interest.

Nonsense, surprise, juxtaposition.

Make lists of potentially useful objects, images, concepts, and actions. Search the list(s) for intriguing combinations.

Will the target audience "get it"?

Is there anything to get?

Consider various styles and methods for rendering the image.

Create a single image.

Create a collage.

Serious, silly, whimsy, nonsense

Odd

Ornament

Surround a photo, illustration, graphic or type element with ornamentation.

Surprise the viewer with an ornate presentation of a common subject.

Add typography that complements or contrasts with the ornamentation.

Photograph an ornate subject and incorporate the image(s) into a design.

Create a dimensional ornament using 3-D rendering software.

Symmetrical? Asymmetrical?

Greek column
Renaissance, Baroque
Laurel wreath, crown, scepter
Sculpture, trophy
Hood ornament

Ornament

ROUGHING IT

An image that is generated using a computer doesn't have to look computer-generated. Many graphics-based programs offer filters and features that allow a designer to mimic pencil, paint, vintage photography, the effects of nature and more.

The following sequence features one of many techniques than can be used to give an illustration a "non-computerized" feel.

The graphic image used in this example was created using Macromedia FreeHand, with effects applied in Adobe Photoshop.

The original "clean" graphic.

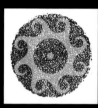

o

A coarse texture is created by applying the "reticulation" filter to a solid color (top).

A high-contrast image is then created using the Brightness/ Contrast adjustment (bottom).

Several layers of the image are shifted, rotated and layered to create a more interesting texture (top).

This texture is then combined with the sun graphic in the "lighten only" mode (bottom).

The next step is subtle: the "torn edges" filter is applied to the outer edges of the circle (top).

The final image is a duotone made from the preceding black-and-white graphic.

Out of Register

Normally, accurate alignment of inks is desirable.

Be abnormal: create the illusion of out-of-register printing by shifting tones or colors.

Would this audience respond better to a misaligned image than to a "normal" one?

Be slightly out of register.

Be way out of register.

Many software programs allow for the manipulation of individual colors or tones.

Out of Register

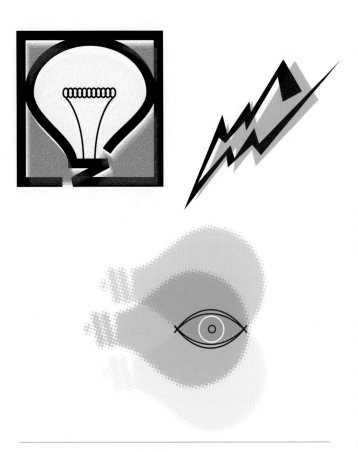

Overlap

Layers of images.

An orderly or disorderly arrangement of elements.

Styles and messages that are in union.

Styles and messages that contrast.

Sequential images.

Stamp or stencil over an image.

Elements could be opaque, translucent
or transparent.

Overlap

Paint

There are endless ways to apply paint.

Paint an image.

Paint over an image.

Use image filters to make a photo or graphic appear painted.

Paint using software.

Paint using paint.

Look through art/graphics publications for ideas and current styles.

Hire an illustrator. Be an illustrator.

Investigate media available at art stores.

Combine a painted image with a photograph or other type of illustration.

Paint

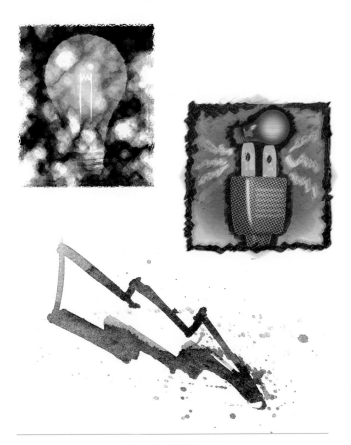

Pencil, Charcoal

Use pencil, charcoal or chalk in a traditional or nontraditional way.

Imitate a pencil or charcoal drawing by applying image filters to a photo or graphic.

Combine a loosely drawn image with a precise graphic or type.

Make final adjustments to a scanned drawing using image-manipulation software.

Illustrate, or hire an illustrator.

Experiment with various tools on a variety of surfaces:

Hard pencil or charcoal	Smooth paper
Soft pencil or charcoal	Rough paper
Chalk	Watercolor paper
Smudge stick	Sandpaper
Eraser	Stone

Pencil, Charcoal

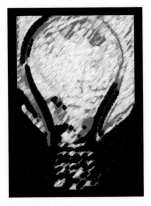

Perspective

Add depth to a two-dimensional image.

Consider different views from which an object could be seen: from above, from below, three-quarter view, close up, far away, askew.

Consider the effect that different camera lenses would have: 35mm, wide-angle, fish-eye or zoom.

Perspective: isometric or vanishing point?

Create an image using 3-D rendering software and explore various views and the effect of different lenses and filters.

Present a series of photographs or renderings of a subject as seen from several viewpoints.

Perspective

Photo Effects

*The samples at right were created from the
same central image using basic image-altering filters.
In some cases, the effect of several filters
was combined.*

Image-altering software and filters are plentiful
and varied.

Keep abreast of developments in this area through
trade magazines, books and investigation.

Explore, experiment, add effect upon effect.

Experiment some more.

Don't allow the effect to overshadow the message
(unless the effect *is* the message).

A mundane image can be made interesting
using filters.

Photo Effects

Photorealism

Use a photograph or illustrate in an
ultra-realistic manner.

Use a 3-D rendering program to create
a realistic image.

Black and white, color, duotone, etc.

Present a subject alone, within a border,
with type or as part of an ornamental configuration.

Photorealism

Repetition

Repetition can emphasize, create pattern, attract interest, imply meaning or add movement.

Repeat a photo, illustration, graphic or type element.

Repeat in an orderly or chaotic manner.

Repeat elements that are alike or different.

Create a backdrop using a repetitive pattern.

Fabric
Wallpaper
Layer
Stack
Neat
Messy

Repetition

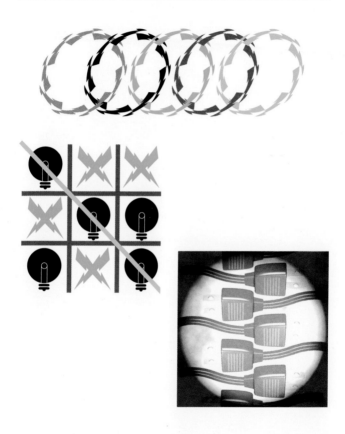

Reverse

Reverse one or more images from another.

Reverse an image from a shape.

Reverse from type.

Reverse from a background image or solid color.

Reverse an image from an enlarged, identical image.

Fill a reversed image with color/tone or
another image.

Styles between images: similar or contrasting?

Reverse

Scientific

Could the message be better conveyed through a scientific or pseudo-scientific portrayal?

Brainstorm the various elements that could be used to impart a look of "science."

Combine a schematic drawing with a photo or illustration of the actual subject.

Add technical text to the image.

Einstein
Mathematics
Astronomy
Chemistry
Blackboard
Chart
Graph
Grid

Scientific

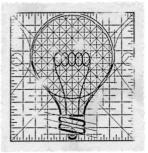

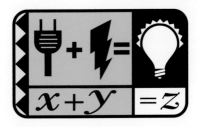

Sequential

Use a sequence to communicate movement, change, transformation or instruction.

Bring an image or object together in stages.

Take apart an image or object step by step.

Transform one image into another.

A sequence could make sense, be silly, be easily followed or require study.

Use photos, illustrations, graphic elements, type.

How many images in the sequence?

Movie frames
Transformation: smooth or sudden
Movement
Cartoon
Film
Slide show
Jigsaw puzzle
Realistic, fanciful

Sequential

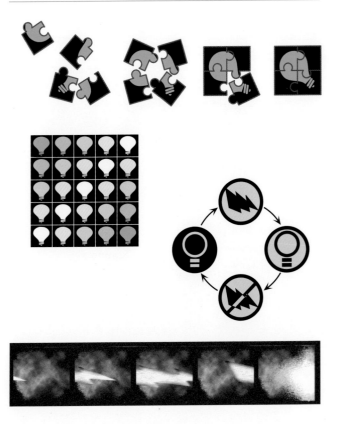

Shape

Reconstruct a graphic image to fit within the boundaries of a basic shape.

Is there a shape that lends itself to an image's presentation and emphasizes its message?

Try different shapes.

Try a simple solution.

Try a complex solution.

Build a graphic from assorted shapes.

Circle
Triangle
Square
Rectangle
Polygon
Multi-pointed star
Ellipse

Shape

Silhouette

Present a subject in silhouette form.

A black, white or colored silhouette.

A silhouette of something real.

A silhouette of something imaginary.

Place a silhouette over another kind of image.

Place a photo, illustration, graphic or type
within a silhouette.

Present a silhouette alone.

Present a group of silhouettes.

Create a pattern of silhouettes.

Silhouette

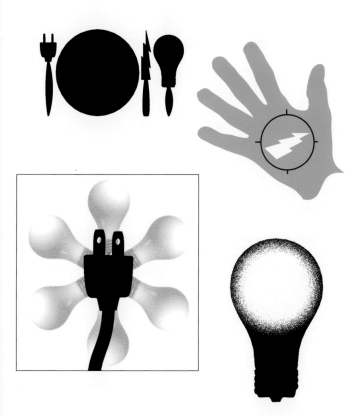

Sketch

Sometimes a sketch or thumbnail is more interesting, or more appropriate, than finished art.

Sketch using pencil, pen, ink, mouse or graphics tablet.

Try sketching on various kinds of paper. Sketch on a napkin, paper towel or bathroom tissue.

Save old thumbnail sketches.

Do many quick sketches before selecting a favorite.

A sketch could be intricate or simple.

Work backward: create a sketched look by applying image filters to a finished illustration or photo.

Combine a rough sketch with sharp, crisp elements.

Sketch

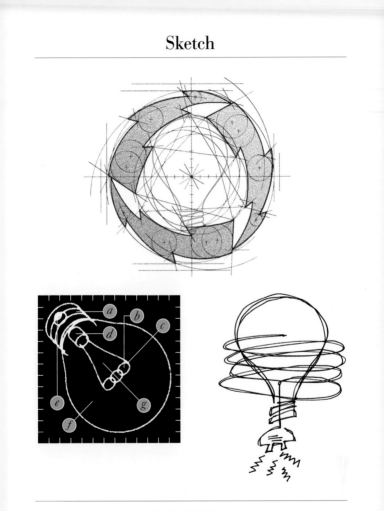

DIMENSIONS

3-D modeling programs take time to learn, but once proficient in their use, a designer can use them to render dimensional images far more quickly than by traditional methods. Additionally, these programs allow for a great deal of experimentation and exploration during the search for an appealing solution.

The sample at right was created using a combination of three programs: Macromedia FreeHand, Fractal Design Ray Dream Studio and Adobe Photoshop.

Examples of how this image could be used as part of a logo are featured on page 222.

The original elements, created in a drawing program.

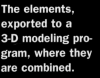

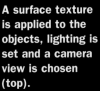

The elements, exported to a 3-D modeling program, where they are combined.

A surface texture is applied to the objects, lighting is set and a camera view is chosen (top).

The rendered image is exported to Photoshop, where areas in need of improvement are treated (bottom).

If desired, additional effects can be added to the image using Photoshop or other photo manipulation programs.

Speak

Give voice to a photo, illustration, graphic or
type element.

Loud, soft, angry, kind, urgent, passive.

Overlay an image with a speaking bubble.

Which voice would best speak the message?
How could this be portrayed?

Would a "thought bubble" be more suitable than
a speaking bubble?

Render the bubble in a style
that emphasizes, or contrasts with,
the style of type within.

Use punctuation marks.

Be serious or silly.

Speak

Spiral

The spiral is an image of continuity and motion that
spans millenniums and cultures.

A spiral can progress in a positive
and/or negative direction.

Spirals within images.

Images within spirals.

Images that spiral.

Spirals as decoration.

Crude spirals, perfect spirals.

Spirals that end quickly.

Infinite spirals.

Spiral

Splatter

Splatter to convey a sense of artistic impulse.

Splatter as part of an image.

Splatter over an image.

Splatter as a backdrop.

Modern art
Accident
Impulse
Black
White
Colorful
Ink
Paint
Blood
Catsup

Splatter

Stamp

Use a stamp to render an image.

Imitate a stamped image.

Stamp over a photo, illustration, graphic or type.

Use a stamped image alone, or use many.

Create a pattern.

A dark, crisp stamp. A faded, worn stamp.

A normal image can be made to appear stamped by altering it with image filters.

Convert a graphic image into an actual stamp.

What about an embossed wax stamp?

Symbol

Every culture has a language of symbols.

Some symbols are cross-cultural.

Symbols within images.

Images within symbols.

Images made from symbols.

Who is the audience?

Which symbols are the most powerful to them?

Pop culture
Spirituality
Crude
Neat
Blatant
Subtle
Timeless
Trendy

Symbol

Tessellate

Tessellate: create a pattern of interlocking, identical shapes.

Some images can be made to tessellate with themselves *(facing page, left).*

Images that do not tessellate by themselves can be contained within shapes that do *(facing page, right).*

Use a tessellating image as focal point, or as a backdrop for other images.

Look at the work of M.C. Escher.

Tessellate

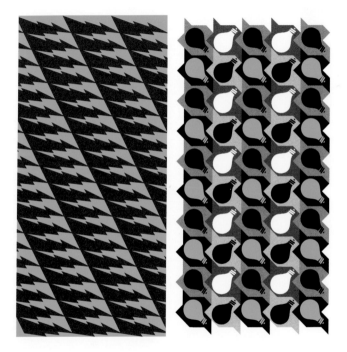

Threshold, Posterized

*Threshold: an image in which the number
of tones has been reduced to two
(most often, black and white).*

*Posterized: an image in which the number
of tones has been reduced to three or more.
Note: When the number of tones exceeds six,
the image begins to lose its posterized look
and appears like a regular halftone.*

Many image-altering programs allow a number
of options in creating either threshold or
posterized images.

This often is a surprisingly easy way to create
a dramatic image.

Feature these kinds of images alone, or combine with
other types of images in a group or collage.

Experiment with color.

Threshold, Posterized

Tonal

Consider using a series of closely related tones within a photo, illustration, graphic or type element.

Colors/tones could be monochromatic (shades of the same parent color), or not.

Consider various color schemes.
Notice combinations that are currently prevalent in magazines, on television, in the theater, and on clothing and recreational equipment.

Which combination of colors/tones is likely to appeal to the target audience?

Computers/software make experimentation easy.

Investigate options.

Explore unlikely combinations.

Tonal

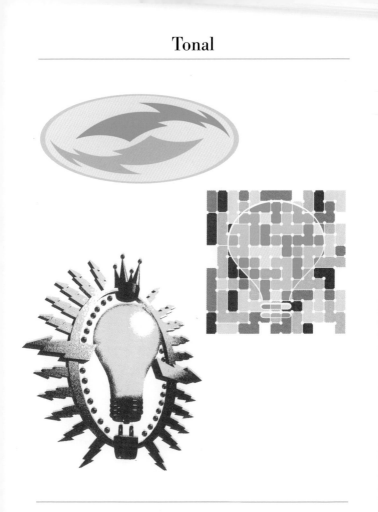

Translucent

Translucent images can create interest and,
if needed, allow other elements to overprint
or reverse clearly.

Experiment with various degrees of translucency.

Investigate the colors/tones that result when
translucent images are overlaid.

Most inks used in offset printing are translucent
and can be used to create color mixes. Beware of
undesirable outcomes.

A light, translucent box or silhouette can be
placed over part of an image to provide a good
backdrop for type.

Layers
Color wheel
Weave
Complex
Simple

Translucent

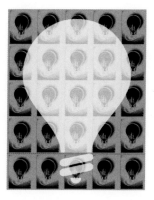

Typographic Element

Use a typographic element to convey or
emphasize a message.

Add typographic elements to an pictoral image.

Construct an image out of typographic elements.

Look at the keyboard for ideas.

! @ # $ % ^ & * ( ) - + = { } | [ ] \ : "" ; ' < > ? , . ~ /

Punctuation marks differ from one font to another.

Which font has the right look for this message?

Typographic Element

"Universal" Symbol

Some symbols carry meaning across
geographic boundaries.

Some styles of illustration convey a
"universal" look.

Universal symbols often instruct, warn or inform.

Alter a well-known universal symbol or sign to convey
a new message.

Transportation signage
Public facilities
International sporting events

"Universal" Symbol

EXPLORATION

Once an image has a reached a certain stage of "completeness," consider different finishing options, then pursue the solution with the most potential.

How is the most promising direction selected, and when is an illustration considered finished? Here is one answer:

An image, developed from a sketch begun on page 66, in need of finishing touches.

At right, four exploratory renderings. The computer lends itself well to experimentation, allowing for a quick investigation of options.

SECTION II

TYPOGRAPHIC TREATMENTS

TYPOGRAPHIC TREATMENTS

Section II of *Idea Index* presents graphic and conceptual treatments that can be applied to logos, headlines, featured text and text blocks. Many of the effects featured in the previous section may also be applied to type, and some of the ideas presented in this section can be applied to pictorial images.

Since this section is focused on the treatment of type rather than on typefaces themselves, a limited number of fonts were used to illustrate the examples. The font families of Helvetica, Futura, Bodoni and Goudy have been used the most often because of their broad functionality, as well as their steadfastness in the midst of changing trends. The font(s) you choose for a project will depend on numerous practical considerations, as well as personal style and instinct.

PRELIMINARY CONSIDERATIONS: FONT, CASE AND WEIGHT

It can be helpful to begin new typographic projects by considering three primary factors: font, case (uppercase, lowercase, upper- and lowercase, mixed) and weight.

FONT. Typeface selection is a skill that requires an awareness of trend, history and audience. There is no right or wrong way to choose a font, but a project's success or failure can depend heavily on the chosen typeface and how it is used. Becoming adept at font selection requires attention to current media and the ability to note both successful and unsuccessful applications of type.

How do effective designers choose fonts? By instinct, really. This "instinct" arises from a practical habit of noticing the way that type is used in current visual media, i.e., print advertising, magazines, television, movies, book covers, packaging, labeling and more.

These designers also take into account the answers to essential questions: Who is the audience for this piece? What typefaces does this audience relate to? Should the font reflect stability, firmness, elegance, action, rage, or...? Should the font be generic and toneless, or should it make a statement of its own? What about compatibility with images and other text? Does the type need to be clearly legible? Does it matter whether or not the font will be out of style in a year? Will the piece be in circulation for more than a year? Which fonts are coming into fashion? Which are going out?

CASE. Once the font selection has been narrowed, it is important to consider how the word looks and functions when presented in different case configurations.

Logos or headlines presented in all caps can convey

formality, power and emphasis. Featuring words in all lowercase can convey informality, friendliness and originality. Presenting a word with the first letter capitalized is often the most "grammatically correct" form. Unusual mixtures of upper- and lowercase letters may be an appropriate and intriguing solution for a particular design problem.

It is worthwhile to look at the word, or group of words, in various case configurations before deciding on the best solution. Often, certain design advantages will present themselves, e.g., better letterspacing, unique ligature opportunities, improved visual balance and/or improved visual relationships with nearby graphics. Use the computer or thumbnail sketches to explore case variations.

WEIGHT. Investigate the visual impact of the word or text when presented in different weights. Many font families offer a variety of weights to consider. Is there a certain weight that emphasizes the intended message? Notice the relationship between the weight of the typeface and the visual weight of nearby graphics and type—sometimes contrast is good, sometimes complementary emphasis is best.

In some cases, a typeface may need to be altered or created "from scratch" to achieve a desired weight.

FONT

WEIGHT

CASE

Upper & Lower   **UPPERCASE**

MIXED   lowercase

Alteration

Add to or alter characters to enforce a message, or to create uniqueness and interest.

Add a meaningful shape, graphic element, photo, illustration or flourish.

Some fonts offer alternative character choices.

Use a single altered letter as a logo or monogram.

Alter a single letter within a word.

Alter the characters of an entire word or sentence.

ALTERATION

ALTER

Backward

Backward type can be used to emphasize
certain messages.

Call attention to a single letter, part of a word, or an
entire word or sentence by printing it backward.

How legible is the backward letter or word?

Is ease of legibility crucial to the audience?

forward backward

BACKWARD

Blur

Blur to convey emotion, emphasize a message or simply to create an interesting image.

Blur all or part of a word.

Blur a little.

Blur a lot.

Push the limits of legibility.

Place crisp type over a blurred image or type.

Investigate the effect of different image filters that blur.

Blur

Border Treatment

A border can emphasize or give new identity
to the type within.

A border can impart humor or tension when
combined with fonts of an opposing style.

Completely surround a letter, word or group
of words with a border.

Partially surround.

Use a single border or several.

A border can help type stand out from an image
or background.

Thick border. Thin border.

Simple. Complex.

Borders, like type, are subject to fashion.

Border Treatment

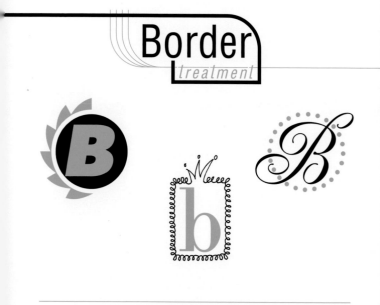

Condense

A condensed font can be used to fit type into a
limited space, or to attract attention.

A non-condensed font can be "squeezed"
with software.

Condense a little.

Condense to the edge of legibility.

Use a combination of wide letterspacing and
a condensed font.

Tightly pack condensed characters.

Create a condensed font for a custom logo
or headline.

C · O · N · D · E · N · S · E

C

condense

C

Conform to Contour

Follow the contour of a shape, letter or object.

Follow closely.

Follow loosely.

Letterspacing often needs fine-tuning after software
has been used to attach type to a path.

Cast the shadow or image of type onto an irregular
surface using photography or software.

Conform to Contour

Crisscross

Break the rules of "proper" typography: crisscross.

Crisscross through a common letter or punctuation mark.

Crisscross by layering words.

Imitate a crossword puzzle.

Vary color, size, weight or font between words.

Use a consistent color, size, weight and font between words.

Crisscross

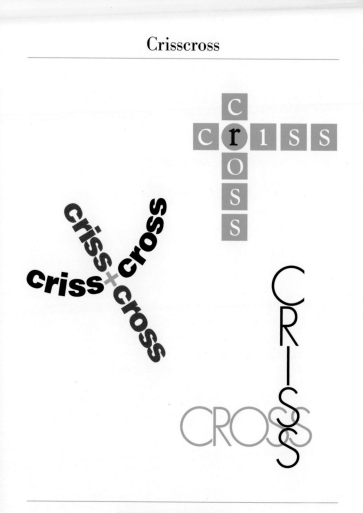

Crop

Crop to enforce a message, or to create interest.

Crop using the border of a shape or image.

Crop using the edge of the page.

Crop into "nothingness."

Crop a single letter, an entire word or
a group of words.

Experiment with degrees of legibility.

Beware of cropping a letter only to have it appear
to be a different character.

*Should the background be allowed to flow into
the cropped letter or word?*

Consider filling a cropped letter or word with a color
or image to help set it apart from the background.

Crop

Crowd

Crowd letters within a word.

Crowd words within a sentence.

Crowd a little. Crowd a lot. Crowd too much.

Crowd letters or words with a border or image.

Crowd or overlap certain letters to improve the overall balance of a word.

Crowd to enforce a visual or conceptual message.

Crowd to attract attention.

How important is legibility to the viewers?

Cultural Connotation

Use a typeface that carries the feel of
a specific culture.

*Which cultural tone(s) could add to the message
being presented?*

Add a cultural symbol to a non-cultural typeface.

Combine the elements of several cultures to create a
worldwide look.

Beware of negative stereotyping and obviousness.

Africa
Asia
Russia
Europe
The Americas
Aboriginal
Hindu
Buddhist
Muslim
Christian

Cut and Paste

Cut letters from paper, fabric, wood, metal or ...?

Imitate cut-and-pasted art using software.

Cut letters or words from printed material and form
a new word or group of words.

Overlay a photo, illustration, graphic or type
with cut-and-pasted type and/or images.

Cut neatly.

Cut irregularly.

Tear.

Paste neatly or loosely.

Cut and Paste

asdjhasdjsaldsaldlsadalsdklaskdlask
dlaskdlksadlsakdasldkasldalsdksadl
sadlsaldjasdljasdlasldasdjhasdjsalds
aldlsadalsdklaskdlaskdlaskdlksadllsa
kdasldkasldalsdksadlsadlsaldjasdijas
dlasldasdjhasdjsaldsaldlsadalsdklask
dlaskdlaskdlksadlsakdasldkasldalsa
ksadlsadlsaldjasdljasdlasldasdjhassj
saldsaldlsadalsdklaskdlaskdlaskdlks
adlsakdasldkasldalsdksadlsadlsaldja
sdjdallsldasdjhasdjsaldsaldlsadals
dklaskdlaskdlaskdlksadlsakdasldkas
ldalsdksadlsadlsaldjasdljasdlasldgffg

cut
&
paste

AN EXAMPLE

Another demonstration of how concepts can be combined to create visual solutions:

In this case, the image of the moon was chosen to accompany the name, "Lunaria," and an effort was made to depict the subject matter in three completely distinct styles.

See also: "An Example," page 40, and "Brainstorm," page 66.

Shape, page 140

Tonal, page 162

Conform to Contour, page 188

LUNARIA

LUNARIA

Damage, Deform

Damage or deform to attract attention, conform to space, emphasize a message.

Alter a single letter, a word, a sentence or an entire text block.

Alter by hand, or use image filters.

Explore the options offered by filters.

Alter the shadow or reflection of type.

Position normal type in conjunction with deformed or damaged type.

Bend	Stretch
Twist	Spherize
Ripple	Burn
Zoom	Explode
Sag	Tear

Doodle

Doodle over type.

Doodle type.

Pencil, pen, ink, crayon, chalk, paint.

Doodle using a mouse or graphics tablet.

Embellish
Enhance
Deface
Serious
Humorous
Goofy

Embellish

Add embellishment to a letter or word(s).

Add embellishment to an elegant font.

Add embellishment to a plain font.

Embellish to enhance meaning or emphasize tone.

Embellish in a crisp, formal style.

Embellish in a crude, spontaneous style.

Swirls
Art Deco
Art Nouveau
Wedding invitation
Royalty
Gild
Ornament
Doodle

Expand

Solve a design problem by using an expanded typeface, or by expanding a normal font.

Feature a single expanded letter as a monogram or logo.

Expand a single letter within a word to convey a message.

Expand an entire word or sentence.

Extreme expansion?

Expand to the point of near-illegibility.

An expanded logotype may adapt well to a particular company's product.

Expand consistently within a word or sentence.

Expand to varying degrees within a word or sentence.

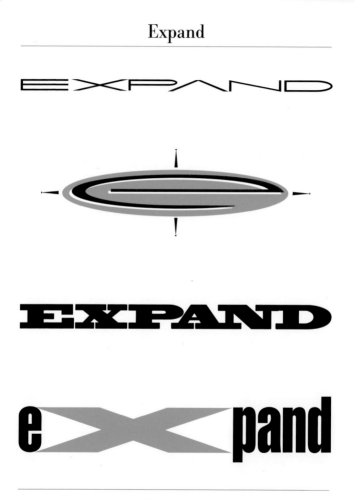

Extreme Letterspace

Letterspace a little, or a lot.

Letterspace specific letter combinations to
improve visual balance.

Letterspace an entire word or sentence to
draw attention.

Experiment with the effect of letterspacing using
various fonts, weights and cases.

Fill the spaces between letters with photos,
illustrations, graphic elements or other type.

Note the effect that letterspacing
has on legibility.

Extreme Letterspace

E X T R E M E

extreme extreme

EXTREME

extreme

LETTER
SPACE

Extreme Size

Impact.

Present the type whole, or bleed off a page's edge.

Print large type over a background color, an image or an otherwise blank page.

Print other elements over a background of large characters.

Position elements inside the negative spaces of large type.

Consider using extremely small type: barely readable.

Contrast large and small type.

Combine this contrast with others: weight, color, tone, style.

Extreme Size

Extreme Weight

Feature individual letters, words, or sentences in an extreme weight.

Heavy or light.

Contrast heavy and light type.

Create custom characters or fonts that exceed upper or lower weight limits of standard fonts.

Contrast the weight of the type with a border of opposing weight.

Combine this contrast with others: size, color, tone, style.

extreme

W

E

W

EXTREME

Gradation

Feature a smooth blend: an airbrushed look.

Feature a coarse gradation: a spraypainted or stippled look.

Gradual? Sudden?

Dark to light. Light to dark. Color to color.

Consider the direction of gradation: up, down, left, right, angled, radial, irregular.

Use consistent or opposing angles of gradation between elements.

GRADATION

Graphic Element

Could the message be emphasized by incorporating a relevant graphic element?

Photo, illustration, graphic element, other type.

Use a graphic element in place of a character, or as part of a character.

Place one or more images within the negative space(s) of a character.

Interweave a graphic with a letter or word(s).

Place a graphic next to or near a letter or word(s).

Use a graphic that has a style compatible with the type's.

Use a graphic whose style contrasts with the type's.

Which should dominate: type or graphic?

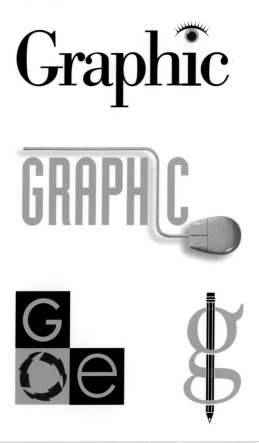

Handcrafted

Create a custom letter, word or font.

Use a font that appears to be handcrafted.

Render with ink, pen, brush, cut paper or...?

Render using software tools.

Create a crude, handcrafted look from an ordinary
font by applying image filters.

Create a uniform style, or a mix of contrasting styles.

Be neat, or not.

Handcrafted

RELATIONSHIPS

Once an image and typeface have been chosen for a logo, it then becomes the designer's job to decide how to arrange the pair.

At right are a few examples of relationships that could be considered for a particular design problem.

Sometimes two or more "official" arrangements will accepted by a client when a single solution will not apply itself well to all common applications.

A demonstration showing how the 3-D star image was created is featured on page 146.

STAR
METALS

Above, the elements.

At right, possible relationships.

Highlight

Bring attention to a particular letter,
word or sentence.

Highlight subtly.

Highlight boldly.

Underline (consider different kinds).

Draw attention with color or tone.

Circle a meaningful letter or word.

Fill a highlighted letter or word with an image.

Reverse a highlighted letter or word from
the background.

Change fonts to highlight a specific word
or character.

Use arrows, outlines or image effects to highlight.

HighLight

HIGHLIGHT

highlight

Human Connotation

Add images of humans, or parts of humans, to type.

Create images of humans using type elements.

Humans doing what?

Position type near or within an image that features humans.

Fashion characters, words or sentences into a human-like form.

Consider the style of the graphic. Does the style complement or contrast appropriately with the font/message?

Person, people
Male, female, unisex
Face, eye, mouth, ear, nose
Senses
Hands, feet
Groups of people
Speak, dance, run, stand, play, work

Image within Type

An image contained within the boundaries of a character, word or group of words.

Which image(s) would best emphasize the message?

Consider a photo, illustration, graphic, pattern or other type.

Repeat an image within each letter of a word.

Use a single image within the characters of an entire word or sentence.

Use different images within each character.

Image within Type

Initials, Monogram

Logo, visual identity, personal icon.

Enclose a character within a relevant graphic element, ornate design, border or shape.

Experiment with ways of linking or otherwise combining letters.

Reverse from, or overprint, an image.

Render a character three-dimensionally, or as part of a three-dimensional object.

Try several fonts.

Which conveys the right feel?

Should alterations be made to make characters "work better" with other elements, or to make them unique?

Inline

Some font families have inline versions.

Inline versions of a font can be created by hand
or by using software.

An inline could be a simple line, an irregular design
or an element that accents a font's style or carries
relevant meaning.

White inline with black type, or vice versa.

Colored inline.

Inlines that vary from letter to letter.

Highlight a character or word by adding an
inline accent.

Interlace

Interlace to create an intriguing typographic solution.

Use the same font between words.

Vary fonts.

Vary colors between words.

Vary baselines.

Vary sizes.

Vary weights.

Create the illusion of letters that interweave
with one another.

Some words can be easily interlaced with each other.
Some cannot.

*Interlacing affects legibility. How important is
legibility in this case?*

Interlace

Label

Label all or part(s) of a photo, illustration, graphic
or type element.

Label with words, letters, numbers, icons or images.

Enclose labels within background shapes.

Allow a label to reverse from or overprint an image.

Label directly on top of an image, or use
lines/arrows to relate a label with its subject.

Label to inform.

Label to create a *look* of information.

Label to attract attention.

Label

Label

1.
2.
3.
4.
5.

Attaching a label to a graphic can be a means of creating visual interest, as well as a way to display information.

Label X
Label Y
Label Z

Line Break

Use line breaks within a word or sentence to
conform to space restrictions, or to create visual
interest.

Be aware of the grammatical rules
concerning line breaks.

Be aware of the rules of legibility and type etiquette.

Defy rules.

Consider using something other than a hyphen
to hyphenate.

Consider changing font, size, weight or color
after a line break.

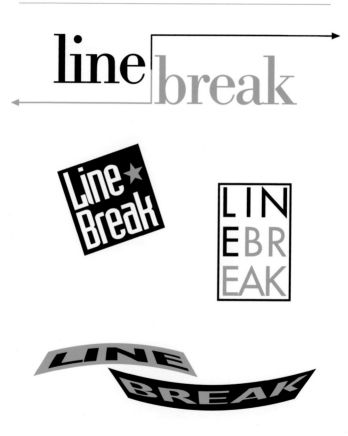

Linework

Use linework to draw attention to type.

Use linework to help type stand apart from
a background.

Use linework that complements or contrasts
with type.

Use linework that adds to or emphasizes a message.

Thick lines. Thin lines.

Dark or light lines.

One line or many.

One weight or several.

Crude or clean.

Create type using lines.

Link, Interlock

Look for ways of linking or interlocking letters to
create balance, or a unique arrangement.

Create a custom logotype by linking or
interlocking creatively.

Link by allowing part of a letter to function
as an element of an adjacent character.

Consider the effect that linking or interlocking
has on legibility.

How easy to read does this need to be?

Link or interlock to the point of questionable
legibility. Consider placing clearly legible
type nearby.

Apply other visual effects to linked or
interlocked letters.

Link, Interlock

LIMITATIONS

Designers are often given tight creative parameters to work within on a project. In spite of this, it can be surprising how much variation there is to be found within limitation.

An example:
A client, "Idea Inc.," wants to see four logo designs that feature a simple light-bulb image (either a graphic silhouette or a photo) and they would like to see this image incorporated into a letterform within the company's name.

These parameters, though restrictive, leave plenty of room for exploration.

At right, four solutions that stay within the given parameters.

Notice how a wide spectrum of graphic styles has been covered by using an array of contrasting typefaces and by featuring the lightbulb in a different letter location for each design.

Mixed Fonts

Contrast brings attention.

Often, more contrast = more attention.

How much attention is too much?

Combine different faces from a single
font family.

Contrast faces from unrelated font families.

What message should the mixture of fonts convey?

Highlight a single letter or word by changing fonts.

Use a different font for each letter of a word or
group of words.

All caps? Upper- and lowercase? Mixed?

Mix other elements as well: tone/color, weight, size.

Develop a "good eye" for mixing fonts by studying
the work of outstanding designers.

Mixed Size

Use a mixture of point sizes within a logo, headline or text to bring attention to a message and/or create visual interest.

Highlight a letter or word by using a larger point size.

Small type can attract attention when presented against a backdrop of very large characters.

Experiment with varying degrees of contrast between large and small type.

Contrast a large, light typeface with a small, bold face.

Contrast a large, bold face with a small, light face.

Vary other factors as well: font, tone/color, weight.

All caps? Upper- and lowercase? Mixed?

Mixed Size

M s

MIXED

[size]

MIXED SIZE

Mixed Tone

Create visual action by using a mix of
colors or tones.

Combine many colors/tones, or only a few.

Combine colors/tones that are closely related,
or widely varied.

Use colors/tones that convey a relevant message
or mood.

Highlight a single letter or word by applying
a different color.

Print single-color type over a background
of varied tones.

Vary both the type and background colors.

Vary other factors as well: font, weight, size.

Mixed Tone

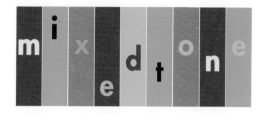

Mixed Weight

Contrast letter weights within a logo,
headline or text.

Highlight a letter or word by using a weight that
contrasts with the weight of other nearby type.

Use a font family that offers a wide range
of weights.

Contrast slightly between weights. Contrast greatly.

Alternate between two weights within a word
or sentence.

Use many weights.

Mix other factors as well: size; font; tone/color.

All caps? Upper- and lowercase? Mixed?

Mixed**Weight**

MIXED
WEIGHT

WEIGHT

Motion

Would a look of "motion" emphasize the message?

Place action symbols adjacent to and/or throughout type.

Present the type itself in motion.

Contrast type-in-motion with static type.

Highlight a letter or word by adding movement.

Add movement to logotype.

Investigate the effect of image filters.

Arrow
Blur
Gradation
Comic-book action motif
Move, stop
Up, down
Left, right
Assemble, explode, whirl, zoom
Bend, squeeze, twist, shake

Odd, Novelty

Use a novelty font.

Create a novel or odd image by combining
unexpected images with type.

Nonsense, surprise, juxtaposition.

Create an image from an arrangement of
typographic elements.

Investigate font catalogs and Web sites for
interesting fonts.

Be subtle. Be bold.

Make lists of potentially useful objects,
images, concepts and actions, then search the lists
for intriguing combinations.

Odd, Novelty

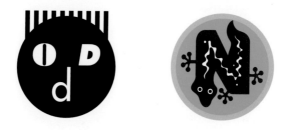

Ornamental Configuration

Surround type with ornate images.

Assemble type into an ornate configuration.

Ornament can be highly flourished, or restrained
and simplified.

Certain styles of ornament are related to a
specific era or culture.

Choose type that complements an ornate border
or background.

Contrast plain type with an ornate border
or background.

Contrast ornate type with a plain border
or background.

Use a mixture of ornate fonts and design elements.

Flourish, embellish, wreath,
Renaissance, Baroque, gold-leaf, era, wedding

Ornamental Configuration

Outline

Use an outline font alone, or create one
using software.

Consider different line weights.

Clean line? Rough?

Add multiple outlines of one or more weights.

Add color or tone to the outline.

Fill outlines with color or tone.

Add one or more outlines that are out of register
with the underlying type.

Imitate or photograph neon signs.

Outline

Overlap

Overlap to draw attention, improve visual balance or create a meaningful typographic image.

Layers of type, or type layered with images.

How many layers?

Overlap letters within a word, words with words or sentences upon sentences.

Vary colors, tones, fonts, styles, sizes or weights between layers.

Order? Disorder?

Create layers of the same image that are out of register with each other.

Paint, Ink

Use paint, ink or painting software to render a typographic message.

Use a font that imitates painted or inked rendering.

Use software filters to make type appear painted.

Hire (*be?*) a calligrapher or illustrator.

Look through current issues of art/graphics publications for ideas and current styles.

Investigate different paints, inks, brushes, tools, paper and fabric surfaces.

Add a painted or inked element to regular type.

Paint, Ink

Observation and experience teach good typographic sense. If you are not already doing it, start taking notice of good and bad typographic solutions: What makes some successful and others not?

Among the fundamentals of good typographic aesthetics is letterspacing. These two pages offer some thoughts and a visual example regarding this important consideration.

When a word is entered into the computer, it is presented onscreen or in print using "default" letterspacing (right, top)—usually good enough for body text, but rarely ready to be featured as a logo, custom headline or other display text. Notice the large amount of "negative space" between the two T's compared to spaces elsewhere (middle: b, c). A more consistent overall tone, achieved through better spacing, would improve the aesthetics of this word form.

To achieve this balance, letterforms need to be altered using graphic software. The type is converted to "paths" (editable images) and portions of the L and T's are cut away to reduce overly large spaces between letters. Additionally, an awkward junction between the letters (a) is smoothed.

Compare the balance of the lower word form with the topmost example: subtle but significant.

LETTERSPACING

Perspective

Create interest by presenting a typographic subject
three-dimensionally.

Take advantage of software that offers
3-D capabilities.

Create type using a 3-D rendering program.
Explore different views.

Consider the effect that different camera lenses
would have: 35mm, wide-angle, fish-eye, zoom.

Consider different views from which an
object could be seen: from above, from below,
three-quarters view, close up, far away, askew.

Feature more than one view of an image.

Combine dimensional type with a flat image or type.

Combine a dimensional image with flat type.

Perspective: isometric or vanishing point?

Perspective

Punctuate

Punctuate to add tone, voice, meaning or
visual interest.

Consider using a different weight for the
punctuating character(s).

Use a different font for the punctuating character(s).

Feature a punctuation mark by itself.

Fill the negative space of a character with
a punctuation mark.

Use punctuation marks as background images.

Look at the keyboard for ideas.

! @ # $ % ^ & * ( ) - + = { } | [ ] \ : " " ; ' < > ? , ~ /

Punctuate!

{punctuate}

Realism

Illustrate a typographic message in a
"realistic" manner.

Photograph or illustrate objects that feature letters or
words, i.e., signage, printed material, building
blocks, letter beads, alphabet soup.

*Are there specific objects that emphasize
the message?*

Use a photograph or illustration of an object that
resembles a letter.

Use 3-D rendering software to create realistic images
that incorporate type.

Consider different materials that the type
might be made of.

*Are there specific materials that emphasize
the message?*

Combine three-dimensional type images
with flat type.

Realism

Repeat

Repeat to fill space, emphasize a message,
create a pattern or image, add movement
or attract interest.

Repeat in an orderly or chaotic manner.

Create a backdrop using a repetitive pattern of
letters, words or sentences.

Repeat a word while changing the font, weight,
case, color or tone.

Overlap?

Apply graphic effects to a repetitive pattern of words.

Repeat

Reverse Type

Reverse type from an image.

Reverse type from a shape or graphic element.

Reverse type from other type.

Fill reversed type with color/tone.

Reverse to white, or allow the background to show through.

Switch from positive to negative type within a logo or headline.

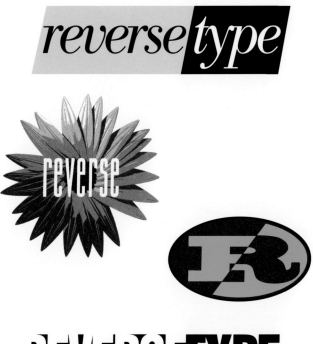

Shadow

Add a shadow to create mood, depth, realism
and/or visual interest.

Present the type itself as shadow.

Reverse type from a shadow.

Cast the shadow of a relevant object over type.

Use a "spotlight" effect to highlight type against
a dark background.

Print the shadow in a surprising color.

Feature type whose form is revealed only
by its shadow.

Create a realistic shadow or use a simple gray tone.

Many software programs feature the ability to add
a cast shadow.

Signage

Feature a typographic message in the form of a sign, or borrow elements from signage.

Which shapes, colors and/or messages could be useful?

Alter a familiar sign to express a new message.

Use a photo, or create images of an actual sign.

Render a sign realistically, graphically or abstractly.

Stop
Yield
Caution
Warn
Inform
Direct

Signage

Speak

Make use of a speaking bubble to give voice to
a letter, word or sentence.

Punctuate?

Use a font that emphasizes the desired tone.

Render a speaking bubble in a style that
conveys a tone of its own.

Loud, soft, angry, kind, urgent, passive.

Which voice would best speak the message?

Place a speaking bubble over a photo, illustration,
graphic or text.

Split Type

Split a letter or word to make room for an image
or other type.

*Should the style of the "interrupting element"
complement, or contrast with, the background type?*

Split to form an interesting ligature and/or to
create visual interest.

How has legibility been affected?

SPLIT TYPE

SPLITYPE

Stencil

Use a stencil font.

Create a stencil font:
bold, thin, serif, sans serif, unusual.

Stencil using real templates. Scan or
photograph the results.

Use a stencil template itself as an image.

Imitate a stencil template using
draw/paint/image software.

Apply color or tone to the inside of a stencil template
in an interesting manner.

Allow a photo or illustration to show through
a stencil's openings.

Be neat or messy.

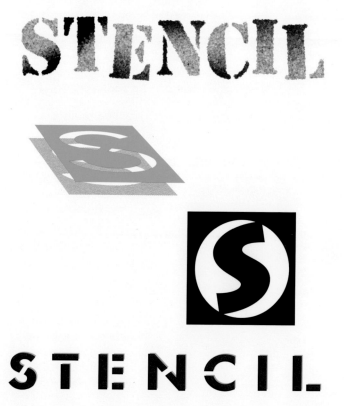

AVOIDING PITFALLS

There are snares in every form of visual media that can reduce the legibility and effectiveness of type.

It is common, for instance, to see the serifs of a delicate typeface fill in when the font is reversed from a dark background at a small size.

At right are examples of three other design decisions that can lead to problems.

Because of its ultra-thin lines, this design will suffer when reduced in size or reversed— the thin lines will tend to break up or disappear.

Extreme horizontal or vertical arrangements can create problems when versatility of use is important.

Besides being somewhat hard to read, this design has another flaw: The size difference between the two words would make it difficult to shrink the design without causing the smaller type to lose legibility.

Tilt

Tilting is a simple means of bringing
attention to type.

Tilt a single letter within a word.

Tilt a single word within a sentence.

Tilt everything.

Tilt all elements at the same degree.

Tilt every which way.

Tilt to follow a shape, or direct attention.

Tilt

Time Period

Emphasize a message by using a font that reflects a specific time period.

Are certain time periods currently in fashion?

Investigate font offerings in type catalogs and on the Web.

Use fonts from a single era, or combine fonts from several.

Complement or contrast the font with graphic elements that reflect a specific time period.

Choose a color scheme that coincides with the font's era.

Ancient Egypt
Roman Empire
Renaissance
Wild West
Old English, royalty
The 60's
Modern, futuristic

Time Period

Time Period

TIME PERIOD

Time Period

Time Period

Time Period

Type with Image

The following three pages feature twelve techniques that could be used to combine text and images.

Note successful and unsuccessful techniques seen in various media.

Combining text with an image often requires creativity, resourcefulness and experimentation.

Try a simple solution.

Explore unique solutions.

Experiment with font, weight, size, color/tone and positioning.

Add a "special effect" to type to help it stand out from an image.

Consider the audience: how easy to read does this type/text need to be?

Type with Image

MASK

OBSCURE

Overprint
or
Reverse

color

Type with Image

Type within Basic Shape

Use a basic shape that fits naturally as a backdrop for a letter, word or group of words.

Alter or arrange type to force it to fit within a shape.

Use a font whose style complements or contrasts with the shape.

Allow type to "bleed" beyond a shape's boundaries.

Highlight a character or word using a background shape.

Place individual letters within shapes of their own.

Try different shapes.

Try a simple solution.

Try a complex solution.

Circle, triangle, square, rectangle, ellipse, polygon, multi-pointed star.

Type within Basic Shape

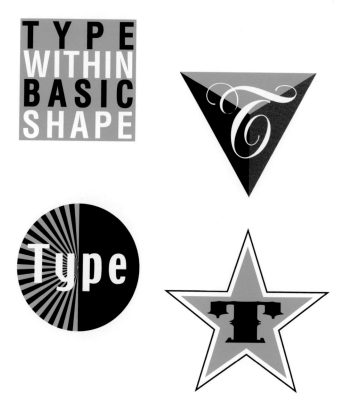

Type within Graphic

Alter or arrange type to fit within a relevant graphic.

Use a font, or create custom type.

Should the type bleed beyond the graphic's boundaries?

Which should dominate: type or graphic?

Use a font whose characteristics complement or contrast with the graphic's style and/or message.

Conform tightly to a graphic's shape.

Float loosely within a graphic.

Type within Graphic

Typewritten

Use a font that imitates typewritten characters.

Use real typewritten characters.

Enlarge typewritten text to accent imperfections.

Consider fonts used by modern digital
output devices.

Antique typewriter
Realistic, imperfect characters
Clean characters
Enlarged text
Computer printout
Cash register
Electronic receipt
Dot matrix

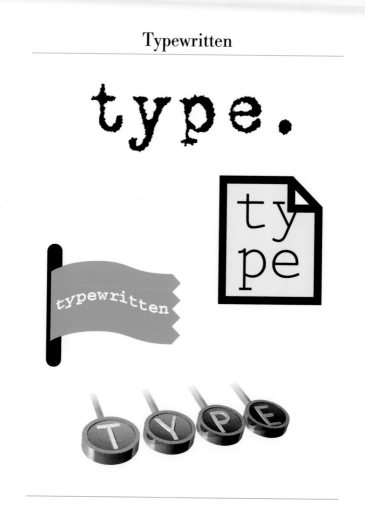

Varied Baseline

Depart from the standard horizontal baseline.

Use multiple baselines within a word to create a
unique logotype or word image.

Allow certain letters to drop, or rise above, an
established baseline.

Make room for graphic elements by altering
a baseline.

Follow a curve, simple shape,
irregular shape or contour.

Create a "wacky" arrangement of mixed baselines.

Varied Baseline

Varied Orientation

Alter the orientation of a single letter within a word.

Alter the orientation of a word within a sentence.

Vary the orientation between a pair of words.

Vary the orientation of every word within a sentence or on a page.

Overlap?

Consider varying other factors as well: font, weight, size and color/tone.

Word Puzzle

Imitate a word puzzle or game.

Form a word from the pieces used in a word game.

Combine word puzzle images with regular type.

Word search
Crossword puzzle
Commercial word games
Secret codes
Missing letter/word games

Word Puzzle

```
Y  S  Q  Z  W  M  N
P  V  J  X  O  W  R
M  U  N  V  R  X  N
T  L  Z  C  D  A  H
R  H  A  Z  V  D  G
B  W  D  E  L  W  P
C  L  K  G  Q  E  H
```

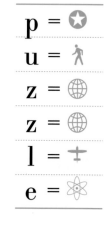

p = ★

u = 🚶

z = 🌐

z = 🌐

l = ✈

e = ⚛

Word(s) within Word(s)

Fill the negative space(s) of a character or
word with type.

Reverse a word from the solid areas of another.

Fill in the negative spaces of a word with a color or
tone and use this space for other text.

Use complementary or contrasting fonts.

Consider varying font, color, weight and/or size
between words.

Legibility?

*I hope that this book will not only
provide additional creative inspiration when
you need it, but that it may also, from time to
time, help you get out of the office
at a reasonable hour.*

Jim Krause

plátano banana

pochas con almejas [almay-Hass] white beans with clams

poco hecho [echo] rare

pollo [po-yo] chicken

pomelo grapefruit

postre [postray] dessert

potaje castellano [potaHay kastay-yano] thick broth

puerro [pwairro] leek

pulpo octopus

purrusalda cod soup with leeks and potatoes

queso [kayso] cheese

quisquillas [keeskee-yass] shrimps

rabas squid fried in batter

rabo de buey [boo-ay] oxtail

rape a la plancha grilled monkfish

raya [ra-ya] skate

redondo al horno [orno] roast fillet of beef

relleno [ray-yayno] stuffed

repollo [repo-yo] cabbage

requesón [rekay-son] cream cheese, curd cheese

revuelto de ajos [rebwelto day aHoss] scrambled eggs with garlic

riñones al jerez [reen-yoness al Haireth] kidneys in sherry

rodaballo [rodaba-yo] turbot

romesco de pescado mixed fish

salchicha sausage

salmonetes [sal-monaytess] red mullet

salpicón de mariscos shellfish with vinaigrette dressing

salsa sauce

salteado [saltay-ado] sautéed

sandía [sandee-a] water melon

sardina sardine

sesos brains

setas a la plancha grilled mushrooms

sobrasada soft red sausage with cayenne pepper

soldados de Pavia [pabee-a] cod, marinaded and fried

solomillo al vino [solomee-yo al beeno] fillet steak in red wine

sopa soup

tallarines [ta-yareeness] noodles

tapas appetizers

tarta cake

tencas tench

ternera [tairnaira] veal

tigres [teegress] mussels in cayenne sauce

tomate [tomatay] tomato

tordo thrush

tortilla [tortee-ya] omelette

tostón sucking pig

tournedó fillet steak

trucha [troocha] trout

trufas truffles

turrón [toorron] nougat

uvas [oobass] grapes

verduras [bairdoorass] vegetables

vieiras [bee-ay-eerass] scallops

zanahoria [thana-or-ya] carrot

zarzuela de mariscos [tharthwayla day mareeskoss] shellfish stew

maíz [ma-**eeth**] sweetcorn

manitas de cordero [kord**airo**]
leg of lamb

manos de cerdo [th**airdo**] pigs'
trotters

mantequilla [mantek**ee**-ya]
butter

manzana [man**thana**] apple

mariscos seafood

mejillones [may-Hee-**yoness**]
mussels

melocotón peach

membrillo [memb**ree**-yo] quince

menestra de verduras
[baird**oorass**] vegetable stew

merluza a la cazuela
[kath**wayla**] hake casserole

mero [**mairo**] grouper (fish)

mojojones [moHoH**oness**]
mussels

mora blackberry

mortadela salami-type
sausage

mostaza [mos**tatha**] mustard

mújol guisado [**mooHol** gees**ado**]
red mullet

nabo turnip

naranja [nar**anHa**] orange

nata cream

nísperos [**nees**paiross] medlars
– fruit similar to crab apple

nuez [nwayth] nut

ostra oyster

paella [pa-**ay**-ya] fried rice
with seafood and chicken

paleta de cordero lechal
[kord**airo**] shoulder of lamb

paloma pigeon

pan bread

panceta [panth**ayta**] bacon

parrilla: a la parrilla grilled

pasta biscuit; pastry; pasta

pastel cake; pie

patas de cordero [kord**airo**]
stewed leg of lamb

patata potato

pato duck

pavo [**pabo**] turkey

pecho de ternera [tair**naira**]
breast of veal

peixo-palo a la marinera [**pesho**
– mareen**aira**] stockfish with
potatoes and tomato

pepino cucumber

pera pear

perdices [pair**deethess**]
partridges

pescado fish

pez [payth] fish

pez espada ahumado [a-
oom**ado**] smoked swordfish

picadillo [peekad**ee**-yo] salad of
diced vegetables; stew of
pork, bacon, garlic and eggs

pimentón paprika

pimienta (negra) [peem-**yenta**]
black pepper

pimiento pepper

pintada guinea fowl

piña [**peen**-ya] pineapple

piñones [peen-**yoness**] pine
nuts

piparrada vasca [**basca**]
pepper and tomato stew
with ham and eggs

piriñaca [peereen-**yaka**] tuna
and vegetable salad

plancha: a la plancha grilled

espadín a la toledana kebab

espárragos asparagus

espinacas spinach

espinazo de cerdo con patatas [espeenatho cay thairdo] pork ribs with potatoes

estofado stew; stewed

fabada (asturiana) [astoor-yana] bean stew with red sausage, black pudding and pork

faisán [fa-eesan] pheasant

farinato fried sausage

fiambres [f-yambress] cold meats, cold cuts

fideos [feeday-oss] thin pasta; noodles; vermicelli

filete [feelaytay] steak; fillet

flan crème caramel

frambuesa [frambwaysa] raspberry

fresa [fraysa] strawberry

fritanga al modo de Alicante [day aleekantay] dish of fried peppers, tuna and garlic

frito fried

fruta fruit

gallina a la cairatraca [ga-yeena a la ka-eeratraka] stewed chicken

gamba prawn

garbanzos [garbanthoss] chickpeas

gazpacho andaluz [gathpacho andalooth] cold soup made from tomatoes, onions, garlic, peppers and cucumber

grelo turnip

guisado de cordero [geesado day kordairo] stewed lamb

guisantes [geesantess] peas

habas [abass] broad beans

habichuelas [abeechwaylass] haricot beans

helado [elado] ice cream

hígado [eegado] liver

higos [eegoss] figs

horno: al horno baked

huevo [waybo] egg

jamón [Hamon] ham

jarrete de ternera [Harraytay day tairnaira] veal hock

judías [Hoodee-ass] beans

judiones [Hood-yoness] broad beans

langosta lobster

langostinos a la plancha grilled king prawns

lebrato hare

lengua [lengwa] tongue

lenguado a la plancha grilled sole

lentejas [lentay-Hass] lentils

liba rebozada [rebothada] sea bass fried in batter

liebre estofada [l-yaybray] stewed hare

limón lemon

lombarda red cabbage

longaniza [longaneetha] cooked Spanish sausage

lubina a la marinera [mareenaira] sea bass in a parsley sauce

macedonia de fruta [mathedon-ya] fruit salad

mahonesa [ma-onaysa] mayonnaise

a vegetable

carne [**kar**nay] meat

carne de cerdo [**thair**do] pork

carne de membrillo [membree-yo] quince jelly (dessert)

carne de vaca [**bak**a] beef

carne picada minced meat, ground beef

carnero [kar**nair**o] mutton

castaña [kastan-ya] chestnut

caza [**ka**tha] game

cazuela [kath**way**la] casserole

cebolla [theb**o**-ya] onion

cebolletas [thebo-yetass] spring onions

centollo [thent**o**-yo] spider crab

cerdo [**thair**do] pork

champiñones [champeen-yoness] mushrooms

chanfaina [chanfa-eena] rice and black pudding stew

changurro spider crab cooked in its shell

chanquetes [chankaytess] fish (like whitebait)

chipirones [cheepeeroness] baby squid

chocos squid

chorizo [choreetho] spicy red sausage

chuleta [choolayta] chop

churros fried pastry strips

cigala [theegala] crayfish

ciruela [theerwayla] plum, greengage

ciruelas pasas prunes

cochinillo asado [kocheenee-yo] roast sucking pig

cocido [kotheedo] stew made

from meat, chickpeas and vegetables

codornices [kodorneethess] quail

col cabbage

coles de Bruselas [koless day broosaylass] Brussels sprouts

conejo [konay-Ho] rabbit

congrio [kongr-yo] conger eel

cordero [kordairo] lamb

corvina [korbeena] fish, similar to sea bass

costillas de cerdo [kostee-yas day thairdo] pork ribs

crema catalana [krayma] crème caramel

cremada dessert made from egg, sugar and milk

criadillas [kree-adee-yass] bulls' testicles; truffles

crocante [krokantay] ice cream with chopped nuts

crudo raw

cuajada [kwaHada] junket, curds

dátiles [dateeless] dates

dátiles de mar shellfish

embutidos cured pork sausages

empanada santiaguesa [sant-yagaysa] fish pie

empanado in breadcrumbs

endivias [endeeb-yass] endive

ensalada salad

escabeche de ... [eskabechay] marinated ...

escalibada flaked cod and vegetable salad (Catalan dish)

escarola endive

ali oli garlic mayonnaise

almejas [almay-Hass] clams

almendra almond

alubias [aloob-yass] beans

alubias blancas white kidney beans

ancas de rana frogs' legs

anchoas [ancho-ass] anchovies

anguila [angeela] eel

añojo [an-yoHo] veal

apio [ap-yo] celery

arenques frescos [arenkess] fresh herrings

arroz [arroth] rice

arroz con leche [lechay] rice pudding

asado roast

asadurilla [asadooree-ya] lambs' liver stew

atún [atoon] tuna

aves [abess] poultry

azafrán [athafran] saffron

bacalao a la catalana [bakala-o] cod with ham, almond, garlic and parsley

becadas snipe

berenjena [bairenHayna] aubergine, eggplant

berza [bairtha] cabbage

besugo bream

bien hecho [b-yen echo] well done

bistec de ternera [tairnaira] veal steak

bocadillo [bokadee-yo] sandwich, snack

bogavante [bogabantay] lobster

bollo [bo-yo] roll

bonito tuna

boquerones fritos [bokaironess] fried fresh anchovies

brandada de bacalao [bakala-o] creamy cod purée

brevas [brebass] figs

buey [boo-ay] beef

buñuelos [boon-ywayloss] light fried pastry

butifarra Catalan sausage – contains bacon

buvangos rellenos [boobangoss ray-yaynoss] stuffed courgettes/zucchini

cabracho mullet

cabrito asado roast kid

cachelada [kachelada] pork stew with eggs, tomato, onion and boiled potatoes

cachelos [kachayloss] boiled potatoes served with spicy sausage and bacon

calamares fritos [kalamaress] fried squid

caldeirada [kalday-eerada] fish soup

caldera de dátiles de mar [kaldaira day dateeless] seafood stew

caldo clear soup

callos a la madrileña [ka-yoss a la madreelen-ya] tripe cooked with chillies

camarones [kamaroness] baby prawns

cangrejo [kangray-Ho] crab

caracoles [karakoless] snails

carbonada de buey [boo-ay] beef cooked in beer

cardo type of thistle, eaten as

MENU READER

Food: Essential terms

bread el pan
butter la mantequilla
  [mantekee-ya]
cup la taza [tatha]
dessert el postre [postray]
fish el pescado
fork el tenedor
glass (tumbler) el vaso [baso]
  (wine glass) la copa
knife el cuchillo [koochee-yo]
main course el plato principal
  [preentheepal]
meat la carne [karnay]
menu el menú [menoo]
pepper la pimienta [peem-yenta]

plate el plato
salad la ensalada
salt la sal
set menu el menu del día
  [menoo]
soup la sopa
spoon la cuchara
starter la entrada
table la mesa [maysa]

another ..., please otro/a ...,
  por favor [fabor]
excuse me! ¡por favor!
could I have the bill, please?
  la cuenta, por favor [kwenta]

Food: Menu Reader

aceitunas [athay-eetoonass]
  olives
achicoria [acheekor-ya] chicory
aguacate [agwakatay] avocado
ahumados [a-oomadoss]
  smoked fish
ajillo [aHee-yo] garlic

albaricoque [albareekokay]
  apricot
albóndigas meatballs
alcachofas artichokes
alcaparras capers
aliñada [aleen-yada] with salad
  dressing